A Soldier's Exp

Southern P

Christian Miller Prutsman

Alpha Editions

This edition published in 2023

ISBN : 9789357964845

Design and Setting By
Alpha Editions
www.alphaedis.com
Email - info@alphaedis.com

Contents

CHAPTER I.

Events preceding my capture—The last day of freedom—A major's folly—My picket line captured—Warrenton—I lose a valuable pair of boots—Culpepper—Farewell to the boots—A disappointing test of good faith.

My enlistment in the service of the United States as a soldier to aid in putting down the rebellion of 1861-5 bears the date, August 2, 1861. I was mustered into the service as a second sergeant of Co. I, 7th Regiment, Wisconsin Infantry, August 28, 1861, which regiment afterwards formed a part of the famous "Iron Brigade." I was afterwards promoted to the rank of orderly sergeant, serving as such until April 15, 1863, when I was commissioned second lieutenant, and finally on May 4, 1863, received my commission as first lieutenant, in which capacity I was serving at the time of the opening of my story.

On or about the first day of October, 1863, after an attack of sickness, I was discharged from the Seminary Hospital at Georgetown, D.C., and ordered to report for duty to my regiment which was then stationed near the Rapidan River, south of Culpepper, Virginia. A few days after I reached my regiment the whole army in great haste started north for Centerville, in order to head off the rebel army which was threatening to get between us and Washington City, *via* the Shenandoah Valley. We arrived at Centerville just in time to frustrate their well laid plans.

On the morning of October 19th, we started out, Kilpatrick's Cavalry in advance, in search of the rebs and found them in full retreat, *via* the Orange and Alexandria Railroad, Warrenton and Leesburg pike, and Thoroughfare Gap. We arrived near Gainesville, where, some months previous, we had fought our first battle. Here we halted a few moments, to mourn over the long mound of earth, which but partly covered the remains of our dead, who on this very ground with our brigade and Stewart's Battery ("B" of the 4th Regulars) had fought the whole of Stonewall Jackson's division for four hours, repeatedly repulsing every attack and holding our ground until, finally, Longstreet's column coming up in our rear, our position became too critical. With Jackson's Division between us and Washington, and Longstreet in our rear, discretion became the better part of valor and we were obliged to retreat, leaving our dead on the field, where this mound now made shift to cover them. History relates that Fitz John Porter had been ordered to check and repulse Longstreet at 4 P.M., and failing to do so was afterwards court martialed, but this is a digression and I must proceed with my story.

Resuming our march south, we arrived at the Manassas Gap Railroad, which we crossed, pursuing our course until we came to a little place called Haymarket, where our division was halted in the fields and a detail sent out for picket duty. Forty of this detail were from my regiment, and I was put in command of the quota furnished from the brigade. We advanced about one mile further south and then west, leaving the roads to be picketed by details furnished from the other brigades of the division.

Hardly had I established my line, and chosen a place for the support to bivouac, before the enemy slipped in at a place called Buckley's Mills, between the picket and the cavalry in our front, and after a short and sharp engagement they forced Kilpatrick's Cavalry to leave the pike and flee to the south-east, in order to pass around the enemy's flank and return to our lines. The corps was compelled to fall back about three miles in order to get north of the rebel army, which was endeavoring by advancing *via* the Bristo station from the east and Thoroughfare Gap road from the west, to get in its rear. The major in command of the lines covering both roads, Bristo station and Warrenton pike, gathered up all the men who could be conveniently reached, and following the corps, left me in ignorance of our dangerous position and entirely at the mercy of the enemy. (This major was afterwards court martialed for conduct unbecoming an officer in the face of the enemy, and dismissed from the service.)

In my position I could hear heavy trains moving on the pike, but could not see them on account of the woods. Finally a couple of rebels, chasing a few sheep, approached our lines, and naturally I undertook to capture them, but failed in the attempt. This revealed our position, and shortly after a long, heavy skirmish line appeared in sight, advancing upon us from the south. I concentrated my line by drawing in my right, which was the most exposed flank, dropped back a few yards in order to give my men the benefit of the timber for protection, and awaited the result.

As soon as the advancing line was within range we poured in a volley by file, confusing and staggering that section directly in our front, but as each flank of their line extended beyond ours and they continued to advance we were compelled to retreat, disputing the way from tree to tree until we reached a point where the Bristo road crossed the pike at nearly right angles; here I commanded my men to rally on the reserve by the left flank, but the men on the left, to my surprise, informed me that the road was full of rebels. I then directed another retreat by the left oblique, in order to get away from the road and make our way back to the fields, where we had left the brigade, but upon arriving there and jumping the fence we found ourselves in the midst of a rebel battery; the rebels had been massing there for more than an hour.

I had no alternative but to surrender. My casualty list was two men wounded, both in their legs. Ah! what a sorry plight we were in. My men were footsore and weary from their hard marching and maneuvering and our animals were completely fagged.

We were gathered in line; I was their first victim, without hat or sword, both of which had been taken away by the first rebel who had approached me.

All and each of the men had shared the same fate.

We heard a few volleys of musketry north and west of us; then spherical case shot from our own guns began to fly among us, which caused the rebs to beat a hasty retreat to protect themselves from the murderous fire of our artillery.

As soon as we reached the pike we turned south and, after marching a couple of miles, we were halted in the woods, and there put in charge of a guard, which was to take us to Warrenton.

It was now getting quite dark, and to add to our wretched condition it began to rain, notwithstanding which we resumed our march to Warrenton, eight miles distant. Upon our arrival there we were put into an old storeroom, which had been improvised as a prison, and in which we found a number of others prisoners who had been captured or picked up from our army on its retreat from the Rapidan.

Those prisoners were crowded into one end of the room, while we were confined in the opposite. The next step was to examine us for boots and shoes. Previous to this I had secretly taken three twenty-dollar bills from my wallet, dampened them in my mouth, flattened them out a little, then slipped them into my watch pocket. But it was not money they wanted; they were looking for footwear.

It was my misfortune to have on a new pair of shop made boots, which I had just received by express from northern Pennsylvania, having been made to order. The provost marshal came in with a small guard and a couple of lanterns and proceeded with his examination. I think I was the first man approached, the officer giving the order, "Examine that man's feet." The order was quickly obeyed. The guards rolled up my pant legs to observe the length of their boot tops and the quality thereof. Their report was "Good." Another of the guard carried an old sack filled with old shoes which had been cast off by men of our army. The officer politely told me "to pick out a pair of shoes from the sack, and get out of them boots." Having no option in the matter I very reluctantly surrendered my new boots, and replaced them with a pair of the cast-off shoes. Later we will hear from those boots. They examined every man's feet, made a number of good trades, then raised the blockade. After this we were allowed the privilege of the whole room, and laid ourselves down for a good night's rest.

Next morning (October 20th) we were marshaled out into the street, put under a mounted guard in command of a lieutenant, and started for Culpepper. This guard proved to be an exception to most guards; they were very gentlemanly, worthy of the responsibility they had undertaken and would frequently dismount and give some one of the poor fagged and footsore prisoners a seat in the saddle. We reached Culpepper about dark, and were ushered into another old storeroom, similar to that at Warrenton, for the night. Here we found the first infantry we had seen since our capture, and were turned over to their charge. The next morning, two other officers and myself were taken across the street to the provost marshal's office and were asked to give our parole not to leave the building, except to look after the welfare of our men when they wanted to report their grievances to the provost marshal, Major Richardson, whose office we were to be permitted to visit. We willingly gave the parole. Major Richardson assured us that our private property should and would be protected, and enjoined upon us to report, for the benefit of all the prisoners, any and all cases of extortion that came to our knowledge.

During the afternoon I observed a good-looking cavalryman stepping around the provost marshal's office, wearing a fine pair of long legged, newly blacked, boots. The thought struck me that those boots were private property and mine, and probably all that I would have to do to regain them would be to report to the major. I did so, and the following colloquy took place:

"Major, I beg pardon, but I believe you made us the promise that our private property would be respected, and asked that we should report all extortions to you."

"Yes, yes, certainly, lieutenant; have you lost anything?"

"Yes, major, I have."

"What?"

"A pair of new boots."

"Where?" was the major's query.

"While in prison," I replied.

"You don't think that I can find them, do you?" he questioned.

"No, sir, but I can."

"Where are they?" asked the major.

"Upon that soldier's feet," pointing to the man with the boots on.

"Ah, ah, that is one of General Stewart's men and I do not have anything to do with him."

This ended both the dialogue and all chance of ever recovering my treasured boots, so I bid a fond farewell to my late pedal coverings, and went back to my quarters a sadder but wiser man. I knew then just how much faith I could pin in the future upon the pledges of my captors.

CHAPTER II.

Libby—Now I lose my money—"Fresh fish"—Quarters and rations—Boxes from home—Two majors escape—A general conspiracy—Bad news and new prisoners—General Butler saves two Union officers by threatening to hang Captains Fitzhugh Lee and Winder—Two female prisoners discovered in male attire in Belle Isle—We secure their release.

After remaining in this prison two nights, we were marched out and south across the Rapidan River, where we found a train of cars awaiting us. We embarked and were conveyed to Gordonsville, where we were taken to the court house for the night. Next day, (October 23d) we were again placed aboard the train and taken to Richmond, where we arrived about 3 P.M.

At the depot we were separated, the enlisted men being taken to Belle Isle, and we three officers placed in the now notorious Libby Prison. The prison was in command of Major Turner, whom I now saw for the first time. He was a very gentlemanly looking man, well dressed and a smooth talker, and assured us he was quite willing to make our short stay with him as pleasant as possible.

After taking our names, rank and regiment, he informed us that the Confederate Government would not allow us to use or even carry United States money; that we would have to deposit our wealth with him for a short time, and that we would be entertained by his brother Dick.

He demanded our pocketbooks, (how thankful I was to know that I had extracted the three twenty-dollar bills and that he was only to get about three dollars) and very deliberately opened them, counted out the money, gave us credit for it in his book, then told a sergeant that stood nearby to search us. Up stepped the sergeant like a man of business, thrust his thumb and finger into my watch pocket and fished out the three twenty-dollar bills. Alas! how soon was my joy converted to sadness! When I saw those bills vanish I knew that they would meet the fate of my custom-made boots.

After serving all alike, we were handed each a chunk of corn bread about one inch thick and four inches square. We then followed the sergeant upstairs, and were ushered into the presence of the other prisoners, where we first heard the cry of "Fresh fish! fresh fish!! fresh fish!!!"

The words came back from every room in the building, of which there were six, and a rush of the prisoners followed the echo, all anxious to get the latest news from our army and the North. We were besieged with such questions as:

"What army are you from?"

"Army of the Potomac."

"Where were you captured?"

"At Haymarket."

"Are they having a big battle?"

"What corps engaged?"

"Have you any news from the Western armies?"

"Is there any hope or prospects of an exchange of prisoners?"

Every one showed the most intense interest and loyalty for Uncle Sam.

Finally the crowd began to scatter and one prisoner came to me saying that, as I was from the Potomac army, I had better go with him to the room occupied by the Potomac officers, which was the upper east room. He led the way and I, following, was shortly installed and assigned in his squad. After posting me in the rules and customs of the prison, my new friend showed me a place near the center of the room where he thought I might find room to lie down that night. He further told me that I would get my rations from him, which would consist of a hunk of corn bread, four inches square by one thick, every morning, and that once a week we would get a meat ration, which would be prepared by the squad cook before being issued.

Night came on and I found a place where I could lay my poor weary bones upon the bare floor, favoring my head a little by using my old shoes for a pillow.

After a couple of days I learned that I might write to my friends, and would be permitted to receive a box from them filled with eatables, bedding, clothing and books. I at once wrote a letter, and in a short time received a well filled box, and was then able to support a bed consisting of a blanket and a quilt. The prisoners also at that time were permitted to send out to the stores once a week and purchase such necessaries as they were able to buy, but like other promised favors this luxury was later denied.

We had among us two chaplains (non-combatants) who were expecting to take the next boat down the river and be put through the lines. When the boat got ready to start their names were called but, not responding to the call promptly, a couple of majors answered to their names and were given a few minutes to get ready, which they did with alacrity. They were soon marched out, went down on the truce boat, and were delivered over to the Union authorities. A few days after the chaplains made another demand for their liberty to the great astonishment of "Dick" Turner, who had to confess that he had "learned another Yankee trick."

After getting acquainted and having my loyalty to the Union thoroughly tested, I was sworn into an organization whose purpose was to overpower the guard, seize their weapons and effect an escape. We were also to receive more guns from loyal citizens, then go to the arsenal and get both guns and ammunition with which to arm the prisoners on Belle Isle, then capture and hold the city until our army from the peninsula could meet us at or near Bottoms Bridge, four miles from the city, and with their assistance, hold the prize.

At that time it was reported that there were nine thousand five hundred men on Belle Isle, two thousand five hundred in the Scott building, (just in sight) and between eight and nine hundred in "Castle Thunder," making in all an army of about twelve or fourteen thousand, though, of course, there were some non-effectives; and, too, at that time nearly ninety per cent. of the men could carry and shoot a gun.

The only difficulty in my mind was to secure arms and ammunition, but we had been informed that they were to be had if we could get possession of the armory. But our plan was soon frustrated, for it was not long before we heard from the negroes that the prison had been undermined.

The next bad news we heard was that Colonel Dahlgreen, who had come within four miles of the city, had been killed on his retreat and a portion of his command captured. The officers captured from his command were brought to Libby prison, and placed in a cell in the middle cellar on the north side, far from light or ventilation. Communication was had with them through a hole in the floor, through which they were also fed by their friends from above.

From this time our luck began to go against us. First the meat ration was stopped; next we were denied the privilege of sending out to make purchases at the stores; then the boxes which arrived for us from our Northern friends were stored away in an old warehouse and we were forbidden access to them. This warehouse was only thirty feet away from us, and, as the boxes continued to arrive, nearly every night, we could plainly hear the guards bursting them open and plundering them of their contents for their own use; another proof of the utter faithlessness of the promises made us by these self-styled "chivalrous southern gentlemen."

The only reason I ever heard given for this change of tactics on the part of our captors was, that they could not negotiate with that "Beast Butler." I learned afterwards that General Butler, who had superseded General Mulford, had, a short time previous to this, notified the rebel authorities at Richmond that he held, as prisoners, Captains Fitzhugh Lee and John S. Winder, and that if they dared as they had threatened, to execute Captains Sawyer and Flyn, he would retaliate by HANGING Lee and Winder. This order had effect in saving the lives of these officers.

At one time during the winter some sanitary goods in the shape of clothing, blankets and provisions, were received and issued to the enlisted men on Belle Isle. Six officers from the prison were taken over to the island to distribute these, and while engaged in that duty they were approached by two rather peculiar looking persons wearing the uniforms of the Union army. They proved to be regularly enlisted soldiers who had been captured with their comrades, as prisoners of war. Upon inquiry it was discovered, or, rather, they voluntarily gave the information, that they were of the gentler sex. This was a surprise that came very near taking away the breath of the officers. They explained how, imbued by a spirit of loyalty to the flag of their country, and being so situated that a disguise was feasible, they had donned the garb of the male sex, eluded the vigilance of the examining surgeon and succeeded in enlisting in the service of Uncle Sam. Up to this time they had kept their identity concealed and had taken part in several engagements as valiant soldiers, but by the fortune of war, were now lying as prisoners at Belle Isle. The treatment received in prison was more than they felt like submitting to, so now they confessed their deception and asked to be released. The officers told them that if they would consent to be released on the ground of being non-combatants, he would make the effort. Their consent was readily given. The next day he reported the case and demanded their release, which was immediately obtained, after which they were brought to Libby, where they remained until a purse could be raised with which to purchase suitable female wearing apparel. They were then taken aboard the truce boat at City Point, amid the "God bless yous" of those who had secured their release. I never heard what became of them, but they said their home was in West Virginia, and that they belonged to a regiment from that State. I have always had a curiosity to know what our Government did for these and other similar cases that were events of our Civil War.

CHAPTER III.

Sick in the smallpox ward—A new plan of escape—Over a powder mine—The plan fails—Filling the roll, one hundred and nine men "short"—Shot at through windows—"Bread! bread!"—Hopes of exchange—May 1st—Boxes which had passed in the night—Brutes—More boxes—Danville, May 8th—Two weeks later, Macon.

By this time my health had become so poor that I was taken to the hospital, which was in the east room on the first floor of the prison. I remained there one night, when it was reported by the surgeon in charge that there were two cases of smallpox in the room and that if I preferred I might return upstairs, which you may be sure I immediately did. Then we were all vaccinated; it did not "take" on me, but there was many a groan for a while from the effects of sore arms.

One night as I lay sick upon the floor I noticed that one of my nearest bedfellows was missing. After a few days he returned early one morning, spoke to his next neighbor in bed and asked him to lie over and give him his warm place in the bed, as he had been on guard for the last four hours and was nearly frozen. His friend, who was Lieutenant Wise, complied with his wish. When he laid down his head nearly touched mine and I heard the man who had given up his warm place (Wise) ask him very secretly how near the end was, and heard the reply, "It is done now; we would have opened it to-night but thought it was too near morning."

Now I had a nut to crack; all thought of sleep was gone and I found myself constantly repeating the question, "Has the time arrived when we are to overpower the guard?"

In the morning I approached Lieutenant Wise for further information, but he was as "mum as an oyster" regarding any intended movement toward escape.

I told him what I had heard him say about the end and he assured me I had been dreaming. But I was not to be so easily evaded, and reasoning with myself that if it were a tunnel which had been prepared it must start from the middle room, the one we were allowed to use from 9 A.M. to 4 P.M. I took my station at the door and was the first to enter the room as it swung open. I could plainly see tracks on the floor coming from the east end and began an examination, but without result. It was plain that I was not in the secret. The day passed—taps were sounded and all retired. An instant later everybody was up, dressing and packing. An Illinois captain came over to me and said:

"Lieutenant, you are not able to make the effort, lie down again."

I mused to myself thus: "What can be the result; if I lie here I may be blown up, if I go and faint by the wayside I shall die, so I may as well be in one place as another." Accordingly I obeyed orders, laid down and in a few moments was entirely alone in that great, cold, desolate and deserted room. My heart fluttered as I thought of the three kegs of powder in the mine underneath me and I tried to keep my pulse still by holding my breath, but it would flutter on in spite of every effort, when, suddenly, even before I realized that any time had passed, there was a rushing of feet and my comrades poured in, one after another, pell mell, hastily unrolled their blankets and stretched themselves on the floor, every man in his place. A moment after, the rebel guard came pushing in with lanterns and scrutinized every man closely. All were apparently sound asleep but me, and most of them snoring loudly. The guard was completely deceived and retired, and then I also fell asleep; but when daylight came I noticed that both my neighbors were gone. I made no comment, though I knew I would have to be counted for them at roll call. I did this by falling in on the right, and being counted, slipped down to the rear of the line, when I was again counted—first time for Wise, then later for his companion.

The count being completed, the adjutant announced that "over a hundred men had answered roll call who were not on the floor."

We began to smell trouble.

The adjutant went downstairs and soon returned with "Dick" Turner and a guard, who drove all of the prisoners out of the room, and then passed them back one at a time, counting them as they filed through the door.

After completing the count they announced they were one hundred and nine men short, and started their patrols out in every direction to recapture the runaways. By noon they had begun to head them off, and in less than three days recaptured fifty-six. The remaining fifty-three were never heard of again as prisoners in Libby; the most of them succeeded in reaching the Union lines.

This escape was hard on the rest of us, however, our liberties being greatly curtailed and our dangers increased. Among other orders, the guard was instructed to shoot every man who showed his head at a window. The first man shot at was Lieutenant Burns, who happened to expose his head too close to an opening in the water closet, where a board had been torn off. Fortunately he only lost half of one ear.

Lieutenant Forsyth of Ohio was not so fortunate. He was sitting four or five feet from the window, reading, when he was observed by a guard patrolling on the opposite side of the street. He fired at Forsyth, killing him instantly, and many other brave officers afterwards shared the same fate as Lieutenant Forsyth, at the hands of those cowardly assassins.

Such was life in this prison, kept by people who prided themselves on their "chivalry." God save the mark!

The month of March dragged slowly along. The commissary boxes which had been sent to us from the north were in sight, but we were never allowed to touch their contents, our only ration still consisting of the one chunk of corn bread daily.

April came, and every day the cry was "Bread! bread! bread!" not only in the prison but also on the streets.

Bread riots were reported to us as having occurred even in the city.

Toward the last of April I was approached by an officer of high rank, who asked if I was "anxious to be exchanged?" Of course I was! I replied, my hopes going up.

He then told me they wanted to send a message north to headquarters at Washington, and I might carry it if they could effect my exchange. The message was that Longstreet's army from Knoxville, Tennessee, about forty thousand strong, had just passed through Lynchburg, going north to join Lee in Northern Virginia; and that Beauregard's army had passed through Petersburg, going north on the same mission, with about thirty thousand men. The message was to be enclosed in a brass button, and they were in hopes they might get me through the lines, as I was in poor health.

The application was made, but alas for the hopes of a prisoner in the hands of rebel captors! I never heard anything further of the proposition, and again settled down to wait some new disappointment.

The first of May came, that day of so many bright memories in my northern home. The city of Richmond was all excitement; old men and small boys could be seen going down Franklin Street with old muskets and clean new white haversacks; and the rebs commenced to issue to us our long-looked-for boxes. Once more hopes of a change for the better took possession of us, and it seemed as if they could not deliver us our boxes fast enough. Negroes would carry them over to the lower middle room and then the roll would be called.

When my name was finally reached I seized my blanket and quilt and got a couple of friends to go with me to the room, where a good large box was waiting to be receipted for. They opened the box, while I spread both blanket and quilt on the floor in great excitement and feverish expectation. They emptied the contents upon my receptacles; next a couple of rebs sat down, each armed with a marline spike made for the purpose, and began overhauling and searching the contents. The salt, sugar, coffee and pepper were scattered all over everything; they reached a roll of butter—think of it, a roll of butter!—and in that the spike struck something hard, upon examination of which they found to be a small glass vial in which had been placed a ten-dollar greenback. No sooner had they laid eyes upon that ten than they appropriated it to their own use. The despised Uncle Sam's money was a very Godsend to them, the cowardly robbers. It is needless to say that I never saw the ten-dollar greenback again. I was permitted to lug my blanket and quilt, with what motley stuff they contained, upstairs, and I studied for some time how to separate the sugar from the sausage, and the salt from the coffee, and I must confess it required some brainwork to so arrange my provender as to make any part of it palatable. Still I finally concluded that I was a lucky man to be even permitted to look upon the relics of the good things that my friends in the north had taken so much pains to send me, and I said again, "How grand it is to be among a chivalric people." On the morning of the fifth the old negro who distributed the morning papers down Franklin Street was heard to cry: "A Great Battle on the Rapidan! Great News from the Rapidan! Full Account of the Battle of the Rapidan!"

My! what an effect this had upon us captives. Our boxes came in thicker and faster until finally old Libby looked like a great storehouse or supply depot, and once more our expectations were raised to a fever heat, only to have them again dashed below the zero mark.

On the morning of the eighth, after roll call, we were informed that an order had been issued for our immediate removal and that we would only be allowed to take one blanket or quilt, which was to be held open as we passed out of the door. We were to receive our rations outside. What a surprise this was to us after all the promises that had been made to us. A perfect bedlam ensued; men would grab up their best books, copies of Dickens, Shakespeare, law books, medical works, magazines, novels, tear out the leaves by the handful and throw the empty covers down on the floor. Next came the groceries, sugar, coffee, pepper, salt, soap, sardines, pineapples and cheese from New York; soused mackeral from Maine; pickled eels from Massachusetts; all sowed broadcast on the floor and mixed into a conglomerate mass a foot or two deep.

We started and at the head of the stairs I turned to take a last, farewell look. I could see many a short piece of candle that had been lighted and stuck fast to the plate which supported the roof, the blaze beginning to lap up the sheeting, but I did not stop to look back again, the outside was good enough for me. I passed down and out through the door, holding my blanket open, and received my hunk of corn bread as I passed out. We started up Franklin Street on the pavement, and, oh, how rough it was after seven months on the smooth floor of the prison. We had bid adieu to old Libby with all its horrors and terrors, yet it proved to be the best prison of my experience.

After marching awhile we turned to the left, then came thoughts of Belle Isle. But, no, we were not destined for that place, for we passed over the bridge, across the island and on to the depot, where we were put aboard some old freight cars. The bell rang, the wheels began to roll, and soon we were whirling over the iron rails. The cars were filthy with dirt, but the atmosphere was fresh, the meadows green and the air fragrant with the perfume of apple and peach trees in full bloom, and I assure you that it was a fragrance we all enjoyed for the time permitted; it was the free air of heaven.

It was the eighth of May and we were moving in a south-westerly course, our destiny being an enigma to us. Late in the afternoon we pulled into Danville, where we were unloaded and marched to a large brick building, which had just been evacuated by other prisoners. Around the outside of the building were a number of Union men, who were just convalescing from the smallpox; scabs were falling off and the men pitting nicely; however, we escaped contagion. We were only confined here about two weeks when we were again put aboard the cars and started south, passing through Charlotte, N.C., and Augusta, Ga., thence west to Macon. Here we left the train and were marched to the fair grounds, which covered about four acres. It was enclosed by a high board fence, with a platform and sentry boxes on the outside for the guard. When we got inside we found one large rustic building near the center, (floral hall) and in the north-west corner was an open shed, fourteen feet wide by over one hundred feet long, which had been built for our predecessors, who in turn had made cots or bunks by driving stakes into the ground about two feet apart, covering them over with boughs and limbs, and leaving just enough room between each one for a man to walk without inconvenience. I was fortunate enough to get one near the center, which was high and gave me a good shelter.

CHAPTER IV.

A tunnel spoiled by the rain—Captain Tabb's cruelties—Corn pone bakers—July 4th squelched—Beyond the "dead line"—Caught—Sherman sixty miles away—Charleston—Negro regimental prisoners—In the gallows' shadow—Whipping-post—Paroles—Money exchange drafts—The Anderson men.

We had been there a few days when I discovered that something unusual was taking place. Every night I could faintly hear the whispering of men engaged in some secret enterprise, but concluded that the best thing for me was to remain quiet and watch. Then came a big rain, which so thoroughly wet the ground that it caused a strip of earth about two feet wide and ten feet long to drop below the surface about ten inches, into a tunnel which these men had been digging. No one *appeared* to notice it, as it was outside of the dead line. The project was abandoned, but the hole under the shed remained intact. Some men who were digging in another part of the prison deposited the earth in this exposed hole, but the guards had "caught on" and were on the watch.

One night shortly after Captain Tabb, who was in charge of the prison, collected about twenty of his guard and, crawling up on the stockade, jumped over the fence and came down on us, swinging his sword, the guard following. They came through under the shed in single file and encircled my bunk and the one opposite, which covered the abandoned hole, and the captain said:

"Now, I have caught you! You will have to pay for this! This is a pretty scrape!"

He called for lanterns and shovels, and, seizing a lantern, held it down under the bunk, saw the hole, stuck the point of his sword down and it happened to hit some of the abandoned tools. He then rose to his feet, turned to Major Pasco, who was on a bunk just to his right, and ordered him to "get up and dig out that hole." The major flatly refused. This raised the ire of Captain Tabb, and he said:

"You refuse to obey my orders, do you?"

"I do," was the calm answer.

Captain Tabb then yelled:

"If you don't get up and dig out that hole you will be shot in less than one minute."

By this time there were not less than eight hundred or a thousand men crowding around so close that the guard could hardly stand. I raised myself so as not to be trampled under foot in case of a rush.

Major Pasco replied:

"I am a soldier of the United States army and a prisoner of war. You have no right to demand any manual labor from me."

Captain Tabb turned to a guard and gave the order:

"Shoot that man. Shoot that man, I say."

The guard brought up his gun, with the muzzle not over two feet from the major's head, and not over three feet from mine, when Tabb cried out again:

"Shoot that man. Shoot that man, I say."

But the guard seemed to know more, just at that time, than Tabb did; for, just so sure as the sun shines, had he obeyed the order not a man of the entire guard would have been left alive. A furious and surging mob were rushing to the front, and at that very instant every man on the guard was covered with some kind of deadly weapon. The guard did not pull the trigger and Tabb so far recovered himself as to not repeat the order.

The next morning while the roll was being called a few negroes came in with the proper tools and dug out the tunnel.

Captain Tabb was intent on revenge, however, and very shortly saw his opportunity. Major Pasco sent out a fine gold watch to be sold and all he received in return for it was eighty dollars in Confederate scrip, when it was easily worth seven hundred dollars at the rate that money was then valued at. When Major Pasco protested he was called out by Tabb, bucked and gagged and made to lie in a hot June sun for three long hours.

When we first arrived at this prison our rations consisted of raw corn meal, one quart each day, besides a very small piece of bacon and some cow peas. We were also furnished with cast iron kettles, which were low and flat, about fourteen inches diameter, and with cast iron covers. This style of kettle I had seen, when a small boy at home, used in a fireplace to bake in. It was then called a "Dutch oven," or "bay-kettle." In these kettles we did our baking by building a small fire both under and over the top. Corn bread now was a necessity of the past, and we all became bakers of corn "pone." I became so expert that by regulating the fire, and placing a slice or two of bacon on top for dressing, I could make and bake a very palatable corn "pone," and one that was pronounced even a luxury. But like all of our former experiences, as soon as we began to think we had mastered one difficulty we found another; in this case our wood gave out and it was a mighty poor "pone" that we could make without fire to cook it with.

Situated in the south-east corner of the prison was just one small spring of water which was good. A half barrel was set in the ground to act as a reservoir for this spring, and this small reservoir was to supply the entire camp of fifteen hundred men with water. As we had to use this water for both washing and cooking, it was insufficient, so we asked for tools and permission to dig a well, which was granted. In a very short time we had a well twelve feet deep, but the siphon that supplied the spring had been tapped, and when the water was used from the well the spring was dry. Then a second well was dug with the same effect as the first, but the two wells proved to be a great blessing to the poor, thirsty prisoners, because, after the exposure of the tunnel, no prisoner was allowed to be outside of the place called his quarters after taps. Consequently during the night both wells made a reservoir that filled up and held the surplus, which otherwise would have been lost.

July Fourth came and we determined to celebrate it in true, loyal fashion. We formed in line and marched around to the front door of the only building on the ground, where we were to hear an oration, to be delivered by an officer standing in the doorway. One of the men resurrected an American flag of small dimensions, three inches by four, but the Stars and Stripes all the same. He fastened it to an old, crooked limb, and elevated it above the heads of the crowd in front of the speaker's stand. We cheered the flag, the first Union flag some of the men standing in that crowd had seen for over two years. No words of mine are capable of portraying the effect the sight of that little banner had upon the crowd. Cheer after cheer rent the air. Hats, caps and arms were raised in the air, tears flowed down the cheeks like rain, and men hugged each other for joy. Never to the longest day of my existence will I forget the scene produced by that little emblem of loyalty, no larger than my hand, as it was brought out from its hiding in that prison. I realized then the full meaning of the Stars and Stripes, and knew why the name "Old Glory" was so appropriate. But, alas, to the utter shame of those in command, our joy was soon cut short, and our intended celebration of the birth of American Independence brought to a sudden and abrupt termination. The rebel guard came in, ordered the small flag to be taken down, dispersed our assembly, and gave the order that if we ever made a similar attempt to show loyalty to the emblem of liberty, they would order the artillery, in plain view to the south-east of us, to open fire upon us and "send us to the kingdom come without ceremony," an order that we well knew would be carried out. We therefore had but one thing to do—to retire to our quarters, and there meditate again upon that glorious, chivalric spirit which so long had been the boast of these representatives of Southern aristocracy.

My health, which had been improving since I had the opportunity to breathe air unconfined by roofs and side walls, as it had been in Libby, was still improving and I made up my mind to attempt an escape on the first opportunity that offered itself. I watched both night and day for an opportunity to steal a boat ride down the Okmulgee River. One morning I was one of the squad sent out after wood, which was dumped in a disorderly pile near the gate. Seeing a hole several feet deep and large enough for me to crawl into, I asked one of the detail to cover the hole over with other sticks of wood after I had crawled in. This was soon done and the detail left with their luggage. It was now only eight o'clock in the morning and I was left outside of the stockade, but still a prisoner in the woodpile near the gate. The day was long and the sun's rays poured down with great heat, and how I longed for a drink of water! Still I was braved to the self-denial, owing to very anxiety to reach the boat undiscovered. But my liberty was not to be obtained in that way. About six o'clock the guard came after its wood and my concealment was at an end. They ordered me out, marched me up to Captain Tabb's office, where I received some unasked for advice, after which I was marched back to the gate and turned in. However, I succeeded in getting a hasty drink of water from the spring, and then had another chance to meditate upon the uncertainty of freedom and the certainty of another long term under close surveillance, before I would again have an opportunity to attempt another escape.

In the latter part of July the Union army, commanded by General Sherman, took possession of Atlanta, only sixty miles north-west of us. A cavalry raiding party came near enough to our prison for us to hear the battle which resulted in their repulse. The cavalry was defeated, some driven away and others captured, the officers taken being turned into the prison with us. Then a new organization was effected to plan another escape, though no definite time was set for the attempt, all that being left to ten of the ranking officers, at whose command we were ready to go and obey orders; but it all ended in such a complete fizzle that I refrain from giving the details.

As soon as the nine days' armistice between the two armies was declared off and Sherman's army, instead of turning and following Hood back north, came rushing toward us, we were put aboard the cars and taken to Charleston, S.C., and there confined in the Charleston jail yard, right under the fire of our own guns. Now we were completely corralled in a small, dirty old pen, without either shade or shelter, save a solemn old gallows which cast a gloomy shadow over us, reminding us of the last victim who had his neck broken by the order of the self-constituted authorities now holding sway with such high hand.

The jail was a large octagonal brick structure, six stories high. In the center of each square was a cell surrounding which was a hall of good dimensions. The building also had an addition four stories high, and in this addition were kept captives from the 54th Massachusetts (colored) Infantry, who were treated with terrible brutality. They were almost naked, and starving, and you could hear their cry of "*Bread!* BREAD! BREAD!" all through the night and day. In the octagonal part of the prison there was also a crowd of peculiar looking half-breeds of both sexes. These were a mystery to me which I never cleared up. All I know is they were turned out in the yard every morning, and there remained until 4 P.M., when they were driven inside again by the turnkey. It was a strange sight and one never explained to us. My theory, however, is that this motley crowd was composed of local prisoners, probably guilty of violating the laws of the community, with perhaps some deserters and runaway slaves. At any rate we saw enough in the conduct of this particular crowd to prove that their rules of morality were away below par.

In order to get out of the mud and free myself from the mosquitoes, I was permitted to occupy one of the old cells at night and sleep on the bare floor, awaiting the regular hour of the turnkey for egress and ingress, and now and then my gaze would be attracted toward the gloomy old gallows, the weight of which (used to swing the unfortunate victim into eternity) was half buried in the ground, where it had sunk after performing its last execution, an additional incentive to melancholy speculation. Upon the next corner north was another large building used for a workhouse; the back part was enclosed by a brick wall and stockade extending around another yard. In the center of this yard a post was set in the ground, and nearly every morning, between nine and ten o'clock, we could hear a whizzing sound, followed by yells. Then we understood; the post was a whipping-post, and the master of the cat o' nine tails was at work upon some victim, in all probability a negro who had been on the street after hours, or guilty of some trifling digression of the rules and regulations of the slave code, as a consequence had been sentenced by the police judge to receive so many lashes on his bare back. We often had to stop our ears, so frightful were the cries of some of the victims of this barbarous punishment, dealt out to human beings for simply exercising a God-given right to think and act for themselves.

After we had been confined in the jail yard for about two weeks, we gave our parole that we would not talk to the guard (which was kept around us only to keep the citizens away), and that we would not leave or go outside of the Marine Hospital or its enclosure. In return for this we were permitted to trade and talk with the hucksters through the palings in front of the building. The hospital was a large three-story brick structure, with basement and the necessary outhouses, including a workshop in the rear. It was entirely devoid of furniture, but clean and comfortable, with plenty of room and good shelter. Wide verandas ran the whole length, both in the front and rear, and shade trees were around the whole building. Our rations too, were improved and we could borrow all the "C.S.S." (Confederate State's scrip) we were willing to carry, if we would give in exchange a power of attorney, properly made out and directed to our paymaster, north. I did not care to do this but many did, and in a short time our yard was full of Confederate money, much to the hucksters' profit. Here are a few of the prices men paid for edibles: Apple dumplings, $3.00 each; yams, $3.00 a quart (one yam made a quart); flour, $4.00 a quart. Eight dollars in Confederate money was given for the promise of one dollar in gold. By this you will readily see that money flew like the wind and it was not long before the supply was exhausted.

The powers of attorney were run through the lines, either by an "underground railway" or by slipping through the blockade. They were presented at Washington, but our Government did not see fit to recognize and pay claims that had been obtained in such manner as had these from the prisoners in rebellious States. The lenders came back, and it is hardly necessary to add that they took no more "powers of attorney." Instead they would and did accept drafts on some bank or "best friend" that had your money for safe keeping. This scheme was worse for the fellows in authority than the powers of attorney, for in many instances the bills were drawn on fictitious banks, located in imaginary places, or on "best friends" who had no existence save in the brain of the man drawing the same.

I, as I said, had taken no hand in the power of attorney fraud, for I was a little afraid it might come to a head and I would be a loser, but when the bill of exchange plan came up I concluded to take a hand. I drew one, of which the following is a copy:

> "CHARLESTON, S.C., August 3, 1864.
>
> "To JOHN CROW, Maconsburg, Wisconsin.
>
> "Please pay to Henry Holloway, or order, one hundred dollars, in cash, and charge the same to my account.
>
> "C.M. PRUTSMAN."

Now, the truth was there was no such place as "Maconsburg" in Wisconsin, to my knowledge, nor was there any friend of mine by the name of John Crow, still that did not hinder the cashing of my order, and in a short time I was the possessor of eight hundred dollars in clean Confederate scrip. As "John Crow," of "Maconsburg," was never found by Mr. Holloway I did not lose anything on my investment. Those who made the "bills of exchange" profited to some extent, however, and the barrels that were delivered to the poor, weak, diseased and starving prisoners, were of great service to them and proved a boon in many instances. It was always a mystery to me why the officers took such chances as they did in letting us have the Confederate State's scrip, but I have often thought they had very little confidence in its real, ultimate value. I also noticed that not one of them ever lost an opportunity to grab Uncle Sam's money when it was within reach.

As soon as we moved out of the jail yard it was used for the Anderson men, but only for one day at a time; then they were marched out to the race course. They generally arrived there early in the morning, were taken out of the cars and held through the day, to be moved through the streets at night, as their clothing was so scant it was not considered decent for them to be seen by daylight.

My first investment with my Confederate scrip was to take one hundred dollars, tie it to a piece of brick and throw it over the wall, from the veranda of the second story, to one sergeant Stetzer, a member of my company and regiment; but the guard heard it strike the ground, drove the sergeant away and pocketed the rags himself. So much for my attempt to relieve the wants of a fellow prisoner. Now, while we lived high for us during the remainder of our stay in that building, the time was very short.

CHAPTER V.

Sherman devastates Northern Georgia—Columbia "Camp Sorghum"—A "dug-out"—I get away—Free—An unexpected plunge—Trouble ahead—Recaptured—A meal—The "debtor's cell" at Abbeville—Back to "Sorghum."

It was now reported that Sherman was on our track, devastating Northern Georgia. Accordingly, on the first of October, the guard was marched in and we were surrounded in the yard behind the hospital. The parole which we had signed was then produced, torn to pieces before our eyes, and declared at an end. We were then marched out, taken to the depot, put into some old dirty cars and transported to Columbia. Here we were unloaded, marched across Broad River, over a long, covered bridge, to an old pasture of about three acres, around which had been ploughed two furrows. One of these was designated the line for the guards beat; the other (inside), the *dead* line. Into this pasture we were herded like so many sheep, without shade or shelter. Our rations were reduced, so that each of us received but a little over a pint of dirty old corn meal a day, and a little sorghum molasses. I had a quart cup and, after washing my meal, had just enough left to make one quart of mush with a sorghum dressing. Think of it, reader, you who have enough and to spare, and have no taste for sorghum molasses, how you would have relished this delightful fare; yet we were forced to accept it by the demands of hunger, and because we were captives to Southern chevaliers.

We named our quarters (the prison) "Camp Sorghum." The commandant, whose name I cannot now recall, was a colonel of the rebel army, and really a kind-hearted man; and I really believe that, had he been able, he would have made our circumstances comfortable; but he was a creature of circumstances and could not control his superiors. He was gentlemanly and courteous to us, and granted us privileges we had never been allowed before; he permitted us to go out to the woods under guard, and gather limbs and boughs from trees with which to make some kind of shelter to protect us from the cold, fall rains. A second lieutenant and myself dug a hole in the ground about three feet wide, seven long and two feet deep, covered it over with limbs and dirt, leaving a small hole at one end to serve as an entrance and exit. This was not original with us, as many similar ones had been made before, nor was it convenient to get in and out of, but by pulling our feet up under us we could manage to keep partially dry and warm.

I was not satisfied, however, and was continually watching for a chance to escape. Finally a long, drizzling rain came on and the colonel gave a number of paroles to some favored, to go out and get limbs, poles and boughs, with which to fix up their quarters, (if you could call their dug-outs quarters). This squad was only allowed to carry its luggage to the guards' beat, throw it over, then return to the woods for more. Then another party was permitted to go out over the dead line, get the truck and carry it back to quarters. I watched them for some time and noticed that the guard did not seem to be very particular about the mingling of those on the outside of the beat. The next time the squad came from the woods I walked out, gathered up an armful of the stuff, returned with the others, and carried the armful to their dug-out. I then waited until they came again, and deliberately walked out with those who went to the timber, the ones who had been paroled for the purpose. I was now outside of the prison in open woods, in plain sight of the pasture and only about three o'clock in the afternoon. This was to be the last trip of the paroled men, so I crawled under the top of a tree, which they had left partly trimmed, and got the men to cover me over with boughs and limbs sufficient to conceal my view from "Camp Sorghum," and there I had to lie on the cold, wet earth, without daring to move, until night.

Night came and the rain still poured down in torrents. I could easily see what few lights were visible in camp and, as I crawled out, turned my back upon these. It was so dark that I had to feel my way, and as I had my back to the camp I had nothing but the sense of feeling to guide my footsteps; but as I supposed the long looked for time had come and I was on my way to liberty, my way seemed easy, and my hopes beat high with a desire to reach the Union lines, somewhere in East Tennessee. In the course of a couple of hours I found an old road which I could follow by means of the small puddles of water that were lying at intervals all along. Then I began to lengthen the distance between myself and camp as fast as my poor, weak limbs and empty stomach would permit.

After an hour or so I began to warm up, but the storm seemed to be increasing as well as the darkness, and finally I lost the road, though still in the woods. I turned and tried to find the road and in the search I soon heard water roaring and tumbling. A few feet ahead I could see a white sheet of water and decided that it was the road. I felt my way carefully along to the edge of the white sheet; there seemed to be a black space between me and the streak of white, which I took to be a ditch that I could jump, when I should find myself in the road again. I made the jump, but alas, the white sheet proved to be a mill pond, which had no bottom at the place where I struck the water, yet I had enough presence of mind to swim for a ledge near the bank. When I reached the ledge, the rocks proved so steep I could not climb them, and I was forced to make my way by clinging to the rocks as best I could along the edge of the water, until I came to a place where some of the stone and earth had been taken away to build a dam. There I crawled out, went up the bank and into the woods again. Then I saw a light streak which I went to and, remembering my former experience, merely followed along its edge until I came to what appeared to be a bridge; this I crossed, and I soon found myself outside of the woods and again in a road. On examination I found the road was fenced and on each side were cultivated fields. The storm was clearing, and I could begin to see. Presently I came to a cornfield; I entered, plucked a few ears of corn and, by cracking a kernel at a time with my teeth, managed to eat some of it; this in a measure appeased my intense hunger. During the remainder of the night I passed a number of houses but for obvious reasons did not seek admission. When daylight came I saw an old log house near the center of a field, which on going to I found to be well filled with unthreshed cow pease. I climbed up to the gable, entered the hovel, dug a hole in the peas, crawled in, covered myself up and there remained through the day, cracking corn and cow peas with my teeth. About an hour after dark I resumed my way. The stars were shining brightly, the road was good and I was leaving "Camp Sorghum" far in the rear, all of which circumstances made me very hopeful indeed. I continued my march through the night, and as soon as daylight approached found a covey in a hedge near a small creek, where I remained through the day with plenty of water to drink. The sun came out quite warm and dried my clothing, and I washed my face and hands in the clear water of the brook, and passed the day without any untoward incident. As soon as it was dark enough I again ventured out and continued my long anticipated journey, passing through what I called a very good farming country.

But trouble was now ahead of me, in spite of all my hopes. As soon as I could see signs of daylight I began to look about for a safe resting place for the day. Seeing a piece of woods not far away I went to it, but upon my arrival I found it to be surrounded by three houses, and very open. Roosters began to crow, dogs to bark, pigs to squeal, and my chances of hiding there without discovery were absolutely worthless. Looking ahead I saw another piece of timber, which looked larger, thicker and more secluded, so I made for it, when to my astonishment I saw a boy approaching on a mule. I stepped behind a tree until he passed, then I continued my way, crossed a road, but had only gone on a few steps when a couple of men stepped out from behind a tree, armed with shot guns, which were immediately stuck into my face, accompanied with the command to "Halt!" Of course I obeyed. They took me in charge and I found myself again a prisoner in the hands of the enemy. One of my captors was a young man, a soldier home on a furlough; the other, an old, nervous, gray-haired citizen, perhaps a neighbor. The soldier walked by my side, was very pleasant and communicative, and the old man walked in the rear with his old shot gun continually leveled at my head, and a determined look, which meant that he would not hesitate to shoot if I made any effort to escape. They conducted me to the soldier's house, and, on reaching it, the young man told the old gentleman that he could go, as he would see that I was taken care of. This seemed to be satisfactory and the old man departed.

The soldier then led the way into the house and I followed. Everything indicated a comfortable farmer's home. I was given a chair in front of the fireplace, in which was burning a good, hot fire. The family seemed to be a large one, and as one after another appeared, he or she would extend a hand, which was grasped by mine in return, much as if we had been old friends just meeting after a long absence. After getting warmed, I asked for a chance to get washed, which was soon furnished, after which I again took my seat by the warm, comfortable fire, but with such a craving appetite that I began to fear I should have to tell my hostess that if she would hold prisoners she must needs feed them, but they had been so hospitable thus far I refrained and waited. Soon after a negro woman brought in a large server on which was a bountiful breakfast, which was placed on the table and I was invited to help myself. You may be sure that I was not long accepting the invitation. I took a chair at the table, the first table I had sat down to in over a year, and enjoyed a clean, wholesome meal.

The lady of the house was a great talker, and while I was eating she entertained me with her views. She told me that before the State of South Carolina seceded they were all a happy, prosperous people; that if they wished to go anywhere all they had to do was to pack their trunks and go. But now they were in the Confederacy, ruled by old "Jeff" Davis, and all the laws they had were laws to impress their property and conscript the men; that all of the best men were being killed off, the only ones left being either deserters or cripples, and that God only knew what would become of them. Her ideas of the future of the Confederacy were anything but flattering or optimistic.

After I had finished my breakfast the soldier told me he would have to take me to Abbeville, and there deliver me over to the provost marshal, the distance being about four miles; but he said that he would not start until four o'clock in the afternoon; in the meantime I could have the freedom of the house and yard by giving him my parole verbally, which I readily did. This soldier and this family were true representatives of Southern chivalry, and had I received the same treatment at the hands of my other captors, all that I have heretofore said in this little story against the false chivalry that prevailed would have been left unsaid. But to proceed: Through the day the ladies of the house repaired my torn clothing as far as they dared, and when the hour of departure came, I was taken in a buggy and delivered over to the custody of the provost marshal at Abbeville jail. Here I was taken to a room called a "debtor's cell," and told to enter. I obeyed the order. Imagine my astonishment on so doing, to behold six other escaped prisoners from "Camp Sorghum." In figuring up the distance which I had traveled in the three nights of my journey, I found that I was sixty miles from Columbia and had traveled on foot and alone, living on corn on the ear and raw cow peas, fifty-six miles, had rode in a buggy four, and had had two good square meals. After remaining in the debtors' room two nights and one day, we were taken out, loaded into an old carry-all and taken to Lexington County court house, where we were confined over night, then started out again next morning, with an entirely different outfit, for Columbia, and there delivered to the provost marshal, who conveyed us in a stylish rig to "Camp Sorghum." The gate was thrown open and I found myself back again in the old quarters, in spite of my ducking in the mill pond, my hard rations of cow peas and raw corn and sixty miles travel. But such is the lot of the soldier and I had to submit. When we entered the camp we were greeted with the old familiar cry of "Fresh fish! Fresh fish!! Fresh fish!!!" but our identity was soon discovered, and, after giving them an account of our experiences, we retired to our various quarters. I found my old dug-out just as I had left it, crawled in and got a good night's rest and sleep, with a good prospect of another long captivity—how long only the future would reveal.

At this time there were many absentees, but all were accounted for at roll count, which we had gotten so systematized that the count was kept correct in point of numbers (one man only was selected to look after the count of the absentees), but the citizens in the country were continually capturing and returning escaped prisoners.

CHAPTER VI.

An "underground railway"—More paroles—Bloodhounds—Bribing the guard—Bloodhound steaks—Two hundred and fifty prisoners "short"—Back to Columbia—Building barracks—A good tunnel started.

I was very secretly informed of an "underground railway," by means of which I could effect a speedy and safe exit to and through the Union lines, were I ever so fortunate as to get outside again. I was to go directly west for twenty miles, then inquire for Colonel —— of such negroes as I might see and they would take me to him; he would put me in charge of a guide, who would pilot me in a roundabout way four or five miles, then put me in charge of another guide to lead me to the next station; here guides would again be changed, each guide to lead me in the secret paths and byways as far as he was acquainted, then leave me with another colored friend and so on until I would be run in to the Union lines somewhere in Eastern Tennessee. Time dragged its weary length along, the commandant of the prison was still granting daily paroles to the men to go out after boughs and limbs until four P.M., each man writing and signing his own parole. At four o'clock the parole was taken up, and the men turned back into the prison by the officer of the guard. But how those "dirty Yanks" were working the paroles. It was so done that every day about as many Yanks were released from the bastile as there were paroles granted.

I will illustrate how this was done: Captain Biggs, of the 147th R.I. Vol. Inft., gives his parole with four others to go out and spend the day; each man gives his parole separately, all to return at four P.M. Now, Captain Biggs has a friend who is aware that he is out on parole with four others. Along about three o'clock a party presents itself at post number one; this post is allowed to speak to the guard. The party enquire for the officer of the guard, who is called, and he steps inside. Then the men approach him one at a time. The first says, "I am Captain Biggs, of the 147th R.I. Vol. Inft.; I gave my parole this morning to go out and spend the day, but we got hungry and came in after something to eat and to get a little rest; now we desire to go back and finish the day." The officer of the guard takes out his pencil and book, then and there takes each man's name, rank and regiment, and goes to the colonel's tent, compares the names with those signed on the paroles, finds them to be correct, goes back to post number one and passes them out. At four o'clock P.M. those who actually signed the paroles go to the colonel's tent, take up their paroles and are turned back into camp, all having been faithful to their pledges. The other five are now outside and left to their liberty. Of course this program is varied to suit the occasion, sometimes one man claiming the privilege, sometimes none, yet enough to average at least two men a day. But the absent men were always accounted for in the morning, by the plan before referred to, some one else counting in their place.

About this time there had been so many stragglers picked up and returned to the prison that bloodhounds were brought forth. Still this made no material difference, the desire for liberty being so strong it merely increased the caution of the men who escaped, without diminishing their numbers. All sorts of things happened in camp. One night a big hog came in and was at once dispatched by the fire of the guard. Another night a cow walked in and after five shots she was disposed of. Another night two men attempted to crawl out, and just as they passed the dead line a light was started in a sick man's quarters. They were instantly exposed to the guard. The story is that they paid the guard a ransom and then were deliberately murdered. I cannot vouch for this as I did not see the act, but I know such things did occur. Shots were often deliberately fired into camp, and no man was safe unless he was in a dug-out. Many of the guard was susceptible of bribery, however, and some of them carried out their contracts. The Yankees educated them, it is said, in this way: A prisoner would approach the guard with an offer to be passed out; the guard would reply, "That won't do, for you know what the consequences will be if I am caught." The Yankee replies, "I will fix that all right; I will give you this gold watch, also two gold rings; you can give the rings, one to each, to the guards on your right and left. When your relief comes on I will crawl out to you, give you the watch and rings, then continue to crawl on a few feet, jump up and run; then you three guards can shoot your guns in the air. I will be at liberty and you will have done all that could be expected of you." This plan is accepted, the prisoner tells a number of his associates, who have helped to make up the ransom, and they wait until the fire is drawn from the guns. Night comes, the relief is exchanged as expected, all crawl near the dead line, the instigator delivers up the treasures, jumps and runs; the guards fire, not only the three, but from other posts adjoining; now the guns are empty and a stampede ensues. The long roll beats, the cry is "Guards fall in," the cannoneers man the artillery, the camp is patrolled and all found to be quiet; the guard retires, and all await daylight. Then the hounds are sent out, the baying commences in the woods west of camp and can be heard for hours. A number of these men are captured and brought back. One man, whom I saw myself, had been bitten in the face, besides having one of his arms almost torn off.

One day two of the hounds took the back track and came into the camp. They only lived long enough to be dragged into one of the quarters, where their throats were cut, their bodies skinned and their flesh cooked and eaten by their captors.

The officials by this time began to think they were not using proper vigilance, and that their method of taking account of the prisoners was not sufficient. So they came in with a strong guard, drove all the men to one end, established a line across the center, and then passed us back over the line, single file, counting us one at a time, as they did at Libby. I was told afterwards that they found themselves short two hundred and fifty men. They searched and probed for tunnels, but in vain; the "parole plan" beat a tunnel all to pieces. Night came on, the guard was doubled, but all was quiet; no attempts were made that night. Next morning we were ordered to get ready to move as soon as possible, and after a few minutes we were marched out and back to Columbia. There we were put into one end of the asylum yard. This was about the first of January, 1865. This yard was inclosed with a brick wall, ten or twelve feet high, and they had made a high board fence across the south end, cutting off about three acres, which was to be our next prison, and into which we were marched. The location was good, with a nice green sod and plenty of good clear water.

The authorities promised to furnish nails, tools and lumber to build barracks with if we would do the work; they to send a mechanic to superintend the first building, which was to be a model for all others. A call was made for carpenters from our number. I was one of many who answered the call. This gave me the first responsibility of any enterprise during my long confinement. The nails and lumber came, also the tools and boss mechanic, who gave us the dimensions of the first house. It was to be 26x26 feet square, eight feet high, with double board crotch roof, a partition in the center and a double fireplace in the partition; the building was to hold thirty-six occupants.

A good, comfortable house was built in short order, and as soon as the outside was done, nails and lumber being plenty, bunks were made, also tables, benches and stools. While this work was progressing I made a scuttle hole to serve as the commencement of a tunnel. It was put down below the surface of the ground about two inches and in the center of the fireplace. Another of the party made a little sled about eight inches wide and sixteen long, the runners rounded at both ends, to be used to draw out the dirt from the tunnel. We surrendered our tools to the next gang which was to build the next house like ours, but before it was completed the lumber and nails gave out and that was the end of the building of the promised barracks. Like all other promises which had been made to us since our captivity there was no fulfillment. So the thirty-six that were housed, including myself, concluded that we would do our part toward aiding the rest, and we very quietly and secretly began digging the tunnel we had started under the fireplace.

One of our party, who was quite an artist with the pencil, obtained permission to go out and make a sketch of the camp, but his real object was to find out where and how long the tunnel was to be. He made the discovery that by crossing under the street, which was about fifty feet, we would open it into a ditch six feet deep, and by going down that a few yards we would come to a draw, with timber on the opposite side, consequently the tunnel would have to be about seventy-five feet long.

The earth was good, solid clay, very hard to dig, but made a good secure tunnel. Our progress was slow, only about four feet a day, and after we had dug about twenty feet a big rain came and the tunnel partly filled with water, but we bailed it out, scattered it over with dry ashes inside, and went to work again. I have seen the guard time and time again come in with picks and shovels and probe the earth right over that hole, but without success. We had dug straight down from the fireplace ten or twelve feet, then began the horizontal part, and for this reason no ordinary probing could possibly detect the tunnel. But that tunnel was not destined to be completed.

CHAPTER VII.

Five of us have a narrow escape from the train—Friendly negroes—A good old "shakedown."

On the afternoon of February 14th we were ordered out, and put aboard the cars, which held seventy-five men each besides the guard. Three men sat in the door with their feet hanging out and others on top.

I now determined to make another effort to escape. I happened to have in my possession a long, wide, thin bladed bread knife, which had been given to me by Lieutenant Dingly of Rhode Island, while I was in Libby prison, and while we were in the Marine Hospital at Charleston I had found an old file. I now took the file and made saw teeth in the back of the bread knife. As soon as we got under headway and outside of the city I got down on the floor and, working the point of my knife through one of the cracks, began sawing a hole through which to escape when a good opportunity should present itself.

After sawing off two planks I began to saw at the other end, but on getting through the first one, I dropped both plank and knife and again I was without means of finishing my work. I sat down over the hole made by the fallen plank and in that manner kept it covered. Before dark it began to rain, night came on and the darkness became very intense. The train came to a stop and I thought I would test the capacity of the hole to let me through. I found I could squeeze through and I dropped to the ground. I then got from under the car to the opposite side from where the guard sat, but found that we were in a cut about four feet high, on the bank of which was a wood pile which I could not climb. Our car was number three, near the light. I at once took in the situation and got back under the car, where I found six others who had followed me out.

We arranged ourselves under the side of the car, just outside of the rails, on the opposite side from where the guard sat. Just then a guard cried out, "The Yanks are a-trying to escape from car number four" (the car directly behind the one we were under). Lighting another torch, a detail of the guard came down the track and we had to get out of sight. Two of the men got back into the car, but the remaining five of us were compelled to crawl under the trucks and lie there. The guard came on, stopped and looked into our car, also number four and, apparently satisfied, reported, "All's well." The bell rang and the train moved on, going directly over us, as we had no opportunity to get from under without discovery, owing to the light from the burning torch; so we hugged the earth while the entire train passed over us. One of the party had his clothing somewhat torn, another lost part of his coat sleeve, but otherwise we were uninjured. The train being now gone, we began to search for some blankets which we thought had been lost in the melee, but while doing this we discovered three men, who probably saw us at the time and, not knowing who we were, ran north; we ran south. We got away from the station, which was called Ridgeway, as fast as we could, and finally stopped to hold a consultation. We decided to go into the woods and stay there until it cleared up enough for us to use the stars to act as a guide, then we would make for the coast north of Wilmington Bay. We, therefore, went into the woods and laid down, but it was so cold we could not stay there, so we got up and began to move to keep from freezing. We went back to the track, then struck the wagon road by the side of the railroad and turned south, one in the advance as a vanguard, the other four following cautiously in the rear. We took turns at being vanguard. When my turn came to go ahead, I had not gone far before I heard voices very plainly off from the road on the leeward side. We came to the conclusion that the road was picketed and that the voices came from the support. It was decided that I must approach the reserve but must not follow the road. So I left the others under a big tree and made a reconnaissance. I started straight for the voices, which were singing; soon I could see lights, which came from three houses now within close distance. I went to each house very quietly, constantly on my guard, and peeped in; I made the discovery that the occupants were all negroes, sitting in front of a big fire that was burning in an old-fashioned fireplace. I knew they were friends, and it looked so warm and comfortable I concluded to go in. I gave a rap on the door, the answer was "Come in," and in I went. They gave me a seat by the fire, and we talked a little about the weather, then I turned the subject and spoke of the war.

They seemed to be pretty well posted and I was convinced their loyalty to President Lincoln could be depended upon. I then told them that I was not a Reb but a Yank. They asked me how I came there. I told them how I jumped from a train load of prisoners, upon which they became very much interested. I began to question them in regard to my safety and as to the danger of betrayal, at which they gave me the assurance that I never would be betrayed by a negro or colored person; and, further, they would both feed and secrete me as far as laid in their power.

Then I told them that I was not alone but had four companions up in the road, who were cold, wet and hungry. Some offered themselves as an escort to go for my companions, and others said they would cook the best they had for us. I accepted their offer and with two of their number went after my comrades, whom I found where I had left them. We all returned to the house again, where they furnished us a supper of hoecake and bacon. We dried our clothes by the fire and, being furnished blankets, lay down in front of the fire for a good night's sleep. Next morning it was still storming, so we could not resume our journey. We were then told that about half a mile from us was a plantation whose occupants were gone from home, and we had better go there to spend the day in the cotton house. They promised to look after our interests. We went and they went with us, but when we arrived there were informed that the master was expected back at noon and it would not be safe for us to remain. Consequently we returned and secreted ourselves under some brush piles where they were at work. Their master lived about twelve miles north, but owned this land and they had come there to spend the winter, cutting cord wood, splitting rails, and piling brush and limbs.

They further stated that the master came there at eleven o'clock on a train which slowed down for him to jump off; that he would stay about one hour, when another train would come along on which he would return home. There were about forty of these negroes, of all ages and sizes from eleven to forty-five years of age. All worked at the slashing, the older ones with the axe, wedge and beetle, the younger ones at piling the heaps.

When they drew their rations they paired off like so many ducks and drakes to prepare and cook the same, each pair composing a mess by itself. After they had eaten their suppers they would have a good time generally, then before retiring they would cook breakfast and dinner for the next day. On the fifteenth, we still lay concealed in the brush piles, each one separate from the other so as not to make a camp that was liable to discovery. The party consisted of Captain Underdown, Lieutenant Moore of an East Tennessee regiment, Captain Ewen, Lieutenant Morgan, and myself from Wisconsin.

When night came we went to the house as arranged and there found the darkies in one of the huts, dancing. After taking a peep through the chinks we entered the large house and were seated. They told us there was a dance in another hut where they were having a mighty fine time. They had a dance every week, but generally came to this house, as it had a floor and was larger, but on account of being afraid they would annoy us they had gone to the other house and were dancing on the ground. We assured them that we would prefer that they would come over to our house that we might see them dance. They dispatched a messenger and in a few minutes they all came swarming in, taking their places on the floor for a quadrille; then an old six-foot darky began to jerk the bow, the old fiddle began to squeal, the caller began his duty, and the dance was on, all keeping time gracefully, and dancing correctly to the call.

Joy was unconfined. After they had danced a few changes Morgan spoke to me and said:

"Prutsman, if you will take a lady and go on the floor and dance, I will."

My answer was:

"Lead out."

He at once presented his arm to "Rachel," a little mulatto of about thirteen years of age, while I followed with one of medium size, about eighteen years of age, so dark that she never had blushed. Lieutenant Moore took third choice, while Captain Ewen closed up the cotillion by leading a large, dusky damsel known as "Rhina Dinah." The set was full and the dance commenced; not to end, however, with a couple of changes, as is the custom now. The changes kept coming; my limbs trembled, and how I longed for the call, "To your seats," that I might get a drink; but those damsels of color proposed to have all the enjoyment possible out of the "Lincum boys," and the caller stood in with them. Finally the cotillion closed with a jig and we seated our partners. The colored folks then took possession of the floor and after a couple of quadrilles invited us to dance again. The invitation was accepted on condition that there were to be but three changes and we again tripped the "fantastic" to the best of our ability. The dance was then at an end, but not the party, for immediately a couple took the floor, facing each other, then another couple took position behind the first; then the lady said to the gentleman: "Can't you catch, can't you catch, can't you catch a squirrel?" This was repeated once or twice, after which the damsel scampered off with the partner after her in a race for life "or a kiss," but it ended in the female being caught and kissed. This was followed up by the other couples in the same manner. I nudged Morgan and told him to lead out again, but he excused himself, saying that he "never would kiss a lady that could not blush." After the kissing party broke up we took our positions on the floor in front of the fireplace to get some sleep.

At daylight on the morning of the sixteenth we were again under cover in our brush piles. The sun broke out from the clouds and sent its rays down upon us. The negroes were chopping and singing as if bedlam had broken loose, and all nature seemed to be having a share in the general jubilee. Soon we heard the booming of cannon and learned that General Sherman was about twenty-five miles south making an attack on the city of Columbia. The negroes took in the situation, and would come to us as they could and tell us that a big battle was in progress at Columbia. At eleven o'clock their master came as usual, but this time he took the whole outfit away with him. One of them got a chance to slip around and let us know that they had to go, but said that if they could they would leave us some bacon and meal in the house.

Night came and two of us went down to the house in hopes of finding something to eat, but there was nothing there. In all probability too close a watch was kept on the darkies, our army now being within hearing. All talk of a trip to the coast was abandoned, but the question was—would the army come to us or must we go to it?

CHAPTER VIII.

Surrounded by rebel forces—Undiscovered—Skirmishing for food—Sambo—Sambo's schemes—Sambo brings succor—At headquarters—Sambo's reward.

The seventeenth came and found us alone and hungry. The brush piles were secure and we spent another quiet day. When night came we could see the city of Columbia burning and we felt that our forces had been victorious. But we were hungry and something had to be done. It was finally decided that Lieutenant Morgan should cross the main road and the railroad, go to the house on the plantation where we had previously been, and seek aid of the negroes there; at the same time Captain Underdown should take a westerly course to a place where we had heard dogs barking and roosters crowing. They both started on their missions. When Morgan got to the road the first thing that caught his eye was the vanguard of the rebel army standing still, but fortunately he escaped discovery and hid where he could hear some rebel officers talking. He gathered from their conversation that they expected to have a big battle at Winsboro, about fifteen miles north of us, but the orders were to camp where they were for the night. Morgan then hustled himself back with the report of his discovery. The rebel army then began to move around on the little flat that lay between us and the road, not over a hundred and twenty-five yards from us, and prepare for camp. In a very short time the little flat along the sides of that little creek was ablaze with fires of an army cooking their hoecakes, while the mules brayed and the drums sounded the tattoo of the drummers. We were in close quarters, but as long as they did not come any closer we were safe.

Now we will follow Captain Underdown: He was an East Tennessean, the oldest of our party, dressed in butternut and thoroughly at home with the Southern dialect. On arriving at the plantation (Gwyn's) he found a man standing by the roadside holding some saddled horses. After watching him for a few moments and being convinced that he was a negro, he approached him. He told him who he was and what he wanted, which was something for five men to eat. The negro at once fell in with the idea, and told him as soon as he could dispose of the horses he would see to obeying the order and request.

In a few moments a man came out of the house with a lantern, which he gave to the negro and ordered him to put the horses, which belonged to some rebel officers, in the barn. The horses were taken care of as ordered, after which the negro took the lantern back to the main house, then went to his own hut, where he stated the case to his "old woman." He then returned to Underdown with the information that there were five rebel soldiers at his house and three rebel officers at the master's. The wife would bake us something as soon as she could, but would have to supply the rebel soldiers first, for as soon as she got a hoecake baked a soldier would take it and put it in his haversack. The rebel soldiers were finally satisfied and took their departure.

The old lady then baked some hoecake and yams and fried some bacon for us. Sambo fetched it out, gave it to Underdown and told him to come back the next night, when he would get something better, as they would cook some chickens for us during the day. Captain Underdown returned to us with the warm "snack," which relieved us very materially from our two days' fasting. We remained outside, watching, the remainder of the night, while the rebel army slept. As soon as daylight appeared we crawled into our hiding places, leaving the field to the enemy, who soon packed up and started off. All day the road was full of marching soldiers, and when night came the banks of the little stream were again occupied with the camp fires of the rebel army.

As soon as it grew dark both Underdown and Morgan went after the promised chicken from Sambo, but there was no Sambo there. His wife came out, however, filled the baskets and delivered them over, saying that if God spared her another day she would cook more and for them to come again; but her heart was full of grief for she said they had taken her Sambo and all the rest of the boys up to Winsboro to work on the fortifications, and that she never expected to see her Sambo again. Underdown and Morgan returned safely to us after passing a number of rebs in the old road; their baskets were full, so after eating a good hearty meal of chicken and other delicacies prepared by the good old darky woman, we promoted Captain Underdown to brevet colonel and quartermaster.

The next morning the rebel army continued to pass along the road and kept it up during the day. We could plainly hear the tramp and talk of the passing column, but kept ourselves carefully concealed. When night came the campers were few in number, and we started our foraging party out again. When they arrived at Master Gwyn's they found that old Sambo had returned. He said that they took him with the rest to Winsboro to work on the fortifications, and, while they were detained in an old warehouse over night, he managed to crawl up through the chimney, out on the roof, then down to another roof, and finally to the ground, after which he took the long walk home and "was mighty tired." Master Gwyn told him he was very glad to see him back, as he needed him, that he had always been a faithful servant and he wanted to keep him as long as he lived.

I will try to give the rest of Sambo's story in his own language. He said:

"Massa telled me dat de Yankee awmy would soon be heah and dat I must take de boys dat am left down in de field and dig some holes in de groun', and dat we mus' bury all de hams and de bacon and de flowah and de groceries and covah dem ovah wid de dirt fust, den wid old dirty straw, den when dey got heah I mus' take de mules and de boys down in de old sage field, wheah de brush is mighty thick down dare. Now, I tells ye, gemmen, when Captain Sherman gets here dese yer niggahs and his boys and dem mules will come out of dem brush; and next dem hams and dat bacon and dat flowah will come out of dat groun' and I tell ye, gemmen, dere will be a great resurwection heah on dat day, ho! ho! ho! ho! haw! haw! haw! haw!" and the poor old slave laughed until the tears streamed down his black cheeks at the thought of this wonderful scheme to outwit his master.

They then gave Sambo a few instructions which were to the effect that, as soon as our army arrived and he could see the Stars and Stripes, he must fetch some of the Union soldiers over to where we were; that he would find us secreted near the middle of the slashing, under the big piles of brush. They then bade Sambo good-night and returned to us. It was now the evening of the twentieth. We could see Sherman's campfires and hear the beat of the drums for retreat, as well as the taps.

The rebs were few in number, but on the alert. Morning came and found us still under the brush piles, but everything outside was amazingly quiet; after an hour or so we could hear a heavy rumbling noise in the air, which became more and more distinguishable, until finally we could hear the talking of a moving army. Morgan crawled close to me, put his mouth to my ear and said:

"Prutsman, we are inside of the Union lines, you can't fool me on that dialect." After listening another moment he said: "I am going out there to see."

My reply was:

"I object; if you cross that flat and it is not our army we will all be sold within two miles of the Stars and Stripes."

He left me to consult with Captain Underdown, saying that if he agreed, he should go. He came back, however, admitting that Underdown had protested, saying he must keep quiet and wait for Sambo to come and deliver us to our friends. In a few minutes more we heard mounted men near us, urging their horses over limb and bush and finally came to a halt. Then a voice could be heard in a sort of a prolonged: "O-o-o-o-o-o-o! O-ho-o-o-o-o-o!"

Then one of the mounted men said:

"Halloo again, they will hear you next time."

Then the voice again resounded, this time as follows:

"O-ho-o-o-o! you five men dat am hid in dat ar brush dare. Why don't you come out? Here am friends; dey have come to protect you."

That voice was familiar, and with a great sigh of relief we came out. There was Sambo with a broad grin on his phiz, and, with him were four of our own men, all mounted on mules. Well, no words of mine can describe the emotion that was exhibited at this sight. We were too overjoyed to express our feelings in words just then. Near by was a squad of Sherman's bummers in command of a lieutenant, whose name I cannot now recall. We gave him our names, rank and regiments, then all went back to Master Gwyn's plantation, where we found a span of mules hitched to a light carry-all. Sambo did not forget the "resurrection," so, after dividing the groceries, hams and flour with Master Gwyn, he packed a good share in the wagon with his family and drove off. We all went to the railroad, where the bluecoats were engaged in tearing up the track, heating the rails and twisting them into knots. We went directly to the headquarters of the Thirty-second Wisconsin Volunteer Infantry, in command of Colonel De Grotte, with whom both Lieutenant Morgan and Captain Ewen were acquainted, and, under the grand old flag of that regiment, we were again breathing the free air of heaven, on soil protected by the Stars and Stripes, and after an imprisonment of sixteen months in the bastiles of a traitorous and revengeful enemy. What a change! We could scarcely realize it. I looked at Old Glory, as she swung to the breeze, and I remembered our feeble attempt to celebrate the Fourth of July on that fateful day when we were charged by the rebel guard and told that we would all be blown to kingdom come if we did not desist at once. How grand that little flag looked then! Now, I could gaze upon the banner of the free, as she waved in the breeze, knowing that this time its full meaning was a reality. Tears ran down my emaciated cheeks, my tongue was paralyzed and my poor weak limbs could scarcely support my body. My mind, so long inured to the hardships of confinement, seemed to be giving away and to be scarcely strong enough to endure the realization of such a sudden and happy change. But, God be praised! we were no longer under the surveillance of those who were trying to destroy the significance of Old Glory, and we felt that time and good food would soon restore us to our normal condition.

While we were still at Colonel De Grotte's headquarters an orderly rode up, presented the colonel with an invitation to Colonel Tilton, commanding First Brigade, First Division, of the 17th Army Corps, inviting himself, his staff, and the escaped prisoners to visit his headquarters. The invitation was at once accepted and we went over, followed by many soldiers and contrabands. After being presented to Colonel Tilton, who received us with great cordiality, and giving our experience very briefly we were again invited to visit the division headquarters, in command of Brigadier General Morrow. Here we were presented to the general and his staff and here we related our experience in the brush piles, and how we were fed by the negroes there and afterwards relieved by Sambo. General Morrow then wanted to know what had become of Sambo and his family. On being informed that they were at Colonel De Grotte's headquarters he at once dispatched an orderly for them (Sambo and family) to come to him. In a few moments Sambo drove up, when the following dialogue took place:

Gen. Morrow—"What is your name?"

Sambo—"Sambo-Sambo Gwyn, sah."

Gen. Morrow—"Did you feed and care for these escaped prisoners?"

Sambo—"Yes, sah, I did, sah, de best I could, sah."

Gen. Morrow—"Where are you going now?"

Sambo—"I am going to follow dat ar flag (pointing to the Stars and Stripes) till I get out ob dis rebel country, sah."

Gen. Morrow—"How are you and your family going to live?"

Sambo—"I have got something in dat ar wagon what we raised ourselves, sah."

General Morrow then sent for his quartermaster and told him to give Sambo a position in his headquarters' train; he then turned to Sambo, instructed him to follow that train and, if he needed any assistance, to at once report to the quartermaster. Sambo raised his hat, thanked him very politely and departed on his mission, a proud and happy man.

CHAPTER IX.

General Logan—General Sherman—Clean at last—General Hobart's hospitality—Luxurious ease—A ghastly reminder of horrors escaped—Washington "short"—Ordered back to my regiment—An honorable discharge.

We were conducted to General Logan's Corps headquarters, were received by "Black Jack" with the same courtesy we had received at the other headquarters, and related some of our experience. Once more we were summoned; this time to see General Sherman. We found the hero seated by a good hot fire, composed of both rails and railroad ties. We were introduced to him and his staff and again made to review some of our late experience while effecting our escape. The general gave us a little talk, then instructed his adjutant general to give each of us a pass which would enable us to pass all guards and all patrols until further orders. The passes being written, General Sherman seated himself at a table, put his own signature to them and we had the pleasure of receiving them from his own hand.

After thanking him from the deepest sincerity of our hearts, we returned to the quarters of the 32d Wisconsin, where we found plenty of hot water and soap, also some extra clothing which had been found in some knapsacks, and right there and then we discarded our vermin filled garments, which had clung to us since our incarceration in old Libby, gave our bodies a thorough fumigating and scrubbing and arrayed ourselves in the new clothing given us, after which we looked and felt more like human beings.

On the morning of the twenty-second, while the regiment was standing in line waiting their turn to march in the passing column, a carriage drawn by a matched team of dapple-gray horses and driven by a soldier, approached and presented us (the Wisconsin escaped prisoners) with an invitation to come to Brigadier General Hobart's headquarters, First Brigade, First Division, Fourteenth Army Corps (The Acorn). We accepted the invitation, took possession of the carriage, and for the next twenty-four days we had the privilege and pleasure of holding down those seats on the line of march, which was almost a direct line northward. At the end of the first day we found General Hobart and bivouacked with his brigade at a place called Black Stock in North Carolina, nearly forty miles from Ridgeway Station. General Hobart, being an old Libbyite who had escaped through a tunnel from the prison in February, 1864, had a warm spot in his heart for us, and the reader may rest assured the welcome he gave us was no unmeaning affair; and the fact that he had furnished the carriage for us on this march gave emphatic evidence that he was fully aware of the hardships which we had been through.

The next morning the corps countermarched back into South Carolina, a distance of fifteen miles, then turned east, leaving the rebel army, which had been massing in our front, far in the rear. The remainder of my stay with that army was indeed pleasant, we were so comfortable in that carriage; besides, when meal time came, we enjoyed the luxuries of the quartermaster's table and every attention was shown to us which could in any way add to our interest and pleasure. At the end of the twenty-fourth day we reached Fayetteville, where we bid adieu to our carriage and those who had shown us so many courtesies. After a few preparations we took a boat for Wilmington.

While waiting at Wilmington for the boat we learned there were about seven hundred ex-prisoners there, enlisted men who were too weak, from their long confinement and sufferings, to be moved north. I visited them, thinking that perhaps I might find some one among them who had been captured with me. On my arrival at the first large warehouse, where a number of the men were, I went in. And what a horrible sight greeted my eyes. Instead of men who should have been in the prime of life and in the full strength of noble manhood I beheld, stretched out on blankets laid over a little of hay, a number of emaciated forms, looking more like skeletons than living beings, their eyes sunk in their sockets, many with no hair on their heads,—all arranged in a circle around the room with their heads toward the wall. I looked with horror upon that scene. I searched for faces, or even one face that was familiar. Alas! they looked at me in utter blankness. I continued my search and in all that number I found but two who could tell me their names, and even those two could give me no definite answer or information other than to name their regiment. My mission was vain, I could not talk to them; and they could no more answer my questions, than if they had been six months' old babies. Some of them could and did laugh; but, oh, such a laugh! It reminded one more of the babbling of an idiot than that of a sentient, human being. They would roll up their eyes at me and stare, then turn them in their sockets until the white appeared, causing indescribable shudders to creep over my frame. And these beings, when taken into custody by the southern "chivalry," were the flower of the best blood and brains in the North. They went forth to do battle for their country and their flag, in all of the pride of intelligent manhood, many of them from the best schools and colleges in the land; others from homes of comfort and affluence, where wives, mothers and sisters ministered unto them with all the love and devotion incident to a sacred home and fireside. They went forth to battle in full command of their strong physical constitutions, only, by the misfortunes of war, to fall into the hands of a set of men who, by all the rights of the best Government the sun ever shone upon, should have been the humane protectors of the fallen foe, but instead thereof had been more brutal in the treatment of their own fellow-citizens, victims of the same misfortunes of war, than had ever been dealt out by the savage Indian tribes of North America, or the cannibal natives of the Sandwich Islands. What a sad commentary upon the teachings that had been inculcated into the minds of the youth of those States, to perpetrate which—the oppression of a down-trodden race—they had rebelled against and attempted to destroy the Government which had been founded to provide homes for the poor and oppressed of all nations. No wonder that God in his wisdom finally overthrew the accursed institutions that were responsible for these atrocities.

After subduing my wrought-up feelings over the sights I had witnessed, I called at the quartermaster's office where I was given transportation on a Government transport to Baltimore and thence by rail to Washington; also an order to report to a certain officer on my arrival at the capital city. On reaching Washington I immediately reported as ordered, but I had to await my turn, being put off from day to day, as there were so many on the list who preceded me. Many of them were the same men with whom I had spent my prison life, who had been paroled and put through the lines and were now settling up their accounts, receiving their pay and getting their final discharge from the United States Government.

On reflection I concluded it would be better for me to see how my own account stood, so I went to the second auditor's office, and lost no time in having the clerks produce the books. I found that I was "short" as follows: "One cone wrench, 30 cents; one cap pouch, 35 cents; total, 65 cents." I produced the money to pay the shortage, but was informed by the clerk that the shortage could not be paid in that way. It then suddenly occurred to me that the aforesaid accoutrements had been lost in action, and I made an affidavit to that effect and my account was at once squared on the books. Since that time I have learned that many an officer was kept out of his pay for no more trifling thing than to be found short in the invoice of accoutrements for which he had receipted. Payment for the same was always rejected until their loss was fully explained. "Lost in action" was the best and easiest way out of the dilemma, and, fortunately for me, it let me out very nicely.

After I had reported to the officer every morning for two weeks, I finally received an envelope. I stepped aside to open it and found, inclosed, an order for me to report to my regiment within the next thirty days. As it happened, I had not been paroled, consequently I was still in the service of the army. The thirty days gave me ample opportunity to visit my friends, and I enjoyed my leave of absence very much. During that short period Lee had surrendered, Johnson was trying to dictate terms for capitulation and—the bloody contest was over.

When the thirty days were up I found my regiment at Burke's station, near Appomattox, from whence we immediately returned to Washington, where I marched with my regiment in review. After that, ten of the western regiments were cut out of the Army of the Potomac, organized into a separate division by themselves and placed under the command of Brigadier General John A. Morrill, formerly colonel of the 24th Michigan. My division reported to Major General John A. Logan, at Louisville, Ky., where we remained for a time, then went to Jeffersonville, Indiana, where I was mustered out of my regiment, July 3, 1865. We then went to Madison, Wisconsin, and on September 15th, I received my final parchment.

I had served three years and eleven months south of the Mason and Dixon line and worn a soldier's uniform for four years and two months. When our regiment was first equipped we were clothed in gray, but later, in common with all other soldiers under the Stars and Stripes, we were given the blue, and that was our color to the end of the service.

While with General Morrill I had the honor of being assigned to his staff and signing my name as A.A. D.C. (acting assistant aid-de-camp), serving in the saddle and on duty. I frequently visited General Logan's headquarters, at Louisville, Ky., and, had the war lasted two weeks longer than it did, I would have received a major's commission. As it was, when I received my final discharge I donned citizens' dress and returned again to the county and state which I had represented with pride and honor, believing that I had only done my duty as a soldier should. I had obeyed orders.

C.M. PRUTSMAN.

Lexington, Nebraska, December 22, 1900.

Milton Keynes UK
Ingram Content Group UK Ltd.
UKHW050923170424
441314UK00004B/196